This book is dedicated to my son Kaylen Gosai.

Little James Visits The Opticians

Written By
Priya Patel.

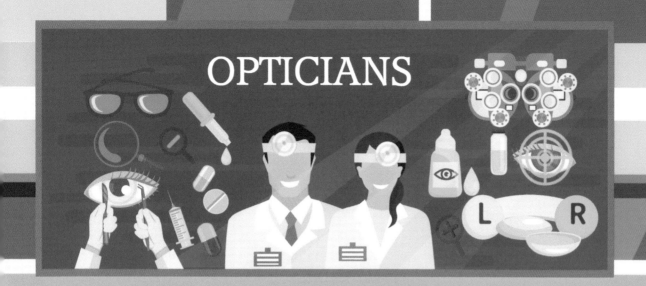

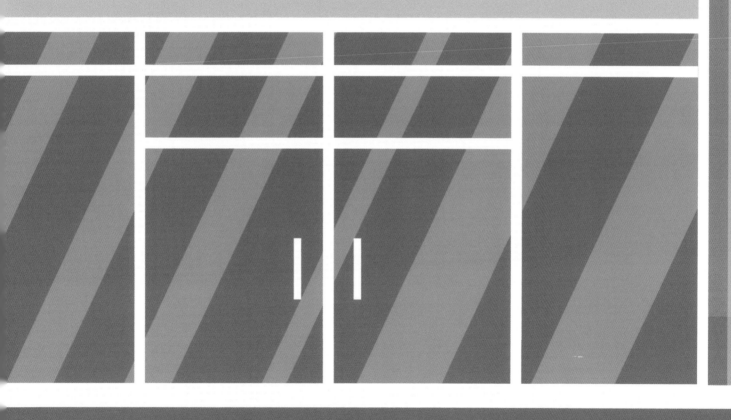

James' mummy signed a form and the Receptionist asked her what day he was born.

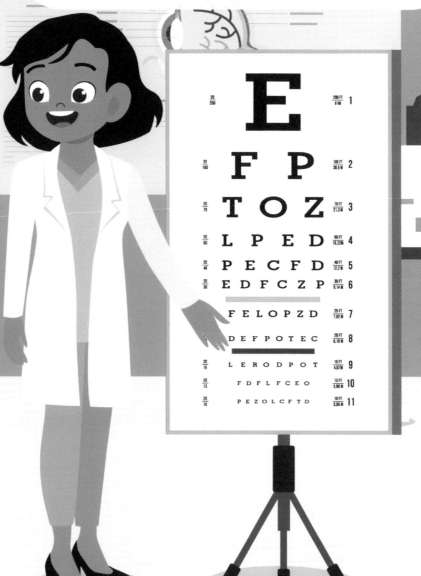

When the test was over a friendly man had to take over. He took James and his mummy to the kids' glasses.

The very next day James put on his glasses and looked out the window. And there was a bus with the number one and a big fat zero. "Mummy! Mummy! I can see the bus and its numbers", shouted James, "and even all of it's vibrant colours".

Priya Patel is a qualified Optometrist,
also a wife, and a mother to a 5 year old boy.
Priya's passion has always been to write,
she completed her education in
Optometry, built a career and started a family.
Now she is embarking on an adventure
in becoming an author, with this being the
first book in a series of children's books.
She hopes her writing can spread
the love and joy within households.

More stories in the series of Little James'
Big Adventures:

Little James Visits The Dentist

Little James Practices Yoga

Little James Learns to Swim

Little James Learns About Nutrition

Little James Goes To The Temple

Printed in Great Britain
by Amazon